W9-AMS-671

Warranty in Zulu

Warranty in Zulu

Matthew Gavin Frank

Barrow Street Press
New York City

©2010 by Matthew Gavin Frank
All rights reserved

Designed by Robert Drummond

Cover painting "How Nature Behaves" (2010)
by Jessica Houston
36" x 30", oil on newspaper on panel

Author photo by Louisa Frank

Published by Barrow Street Press
Distributed by:
Barrow Street
P.O. Box 1831
Murray Hill Station
New York, NY 10156

First Edition

Library of Congress control number: 2010931726

ISBN 978-09819876-3-7

For Baba

CONTENTS

In Burying the Avocet

The skeleton of an avocet erupts
in a cigar box. A fire

like cognac. Like the avocet.
I have trouble choosing: worm

or sleep. Luckily,
I am not long-legged.

This morning, I told my wife
my belt was an eel, coming to surface

for the sheen of the snaps, for what might
be hidden in the shores

of the back pocket. She told me
a joke in Portuguese, about the avocet

who ate the eel and turned into
a flying fish. It's funnier

in Portuguese. In this language,
we build our coffins like homes—

the purple drapes here, the dinette set . . .
The avocet is a female apricot,

she says, the burial is a long
slow look at a solemn channel—

before the shovels, streaked with the leavings
of *omuboro* cherry, allow

for rain. I told my wife,
if I worked at the graveyard,

I would also try to knock the fruit
from the tree. She tells me

the joke about yellow feet
and other signs. How

to bury the bird
is to choose between two unknowables.

Flight, death. We only think
that she's the one we've been spooning with.

In the creased lid
of the cigar box is only

the aching of paper, and a punchline:
how the armless man

lives with itch. This
is who we have to live with.

Four Hours to Mpumalanga

In Bulawayo, three Ndebele women burn the dead
with lamb fat. The gasoline went south
months ago: The waterbuck sips to feed
the leopard.

In Burgersfort, Christmas, and the people's
shirts break like sculpture, shards of discipline
and yellow. A man holds his bottle of Klipdrift
two kilometers from the cashier,
while a heavy old woman tries
to sell him her great-granddaughter. Everywhere,
sweat, and her voice.

Try not to imagine the dead, one country
away, running to candle wax a whole township.
We must open our presents, spin the sheep
over the spit.

Brandy will save us through evening,
quiet us, give life to the beetles and *shongololo*
centipedes, thick as our wrists.

If we can't drive, we eat what we find.
In the orange farm, the defunct baboons, still
as oil paint, pant the crops into life,
boys who sell ears of corn
at the intersection, as a pastime,
scratching their weakest shoulders
to the tissue.

We eat not to see every museum
in Stellenbosch, where the joints of all hated art
crack their importance into the corners
of a dovetailing crate.

Father-in-Law Agitprop

It's before coffee and after everything else.
A Sotho policewoman waves us to the side

of the road with a flashlight. One hundred kilometers
behind us, Johannesburg goes to sleep. Corn,

purple, orange, weapon. Johann says,
Here, an hour in a cell is a death sentence.

He pulls his hands from the steering wheel,
lips trying to close over the end of a Peter

Stuyvesant. Handcuffs. A pig on a spit.
Gumboots in a souvenir shop. How quickly

we would sell our misery and our love. History
is this ear of corn, and this Giant Kingfisher,

licking blood from an eel. His wings
mock the Southern Cross and I pray

for Andromeda. The policewoman speaks
in mirrors, almost in retrospect,

side-views. Her wings
bury our brandies

with Johann's 100-rand note.
We will live today

to change our socks
and lower the parking brake,

this time, as if, into the earth.

Khayelitsha Township

You've never seen this before. Fourteen of us
crowded around the paintbox, in the middle
of our rugby game, posing for a white man's

picture. His daughter goes to Christian school
outside Burgersfort, where she learns to call us
strangers. It's nicer, funny because you've never

heard us resume our games, shout, smile,
seen my grandmother allowed a house,
corrugated iron, mangowood, three red

onion sacks. The police don't knock it over
anymore. Some of them now are from town.
Ashley tells us that, outside, they charge us

ten cents for plastic bags.
Sometimes, a tour bus comes in,
the people lower their windows and point

their cameras. Ashley says, our pictures
are now on calendars they sell at the airport.
I have to tell you: Fridays we go to the faucet,

a three-hour-and-twenty-minute line,
and Katie finds a coin. The picture man
maybe, or dropped from the can, the collection

for the cornmeal. She takes it because she's
too young, and I'm too old to tell her better.
Her hand knots in mine, purple, orange.

We're a little hungry, but we're clean
until the rain comes.

The last flood, Katie swam to the paintbox,
climbed to the top, wrote *WIN* in silver ink.

Favor

You say: *Never shake a can*
of peas. There's no honor in crushing
fifty green hemispheres into meal. But sometimes,

I wish the old constellations would return
from the dead, just to go soft,
green in my fingers. And of what is a hemisphere

made? Sometimes, in Ohrigstad,
the market scares me. When the light
catches the *atchar* bottle, I can hear
the mangoes screaming.

Other times, the housemaid's hair-dye
clots like blood, her four children
hiding their pillows in the toolshed, eating

the peas your mother leaves over.
Because you were born here,
you're used to this. But I should tell you:

That thing under your bed is not
a real goblin, and a pile of toenails
can't kill you. Not now anyway.

A decade ago, death might have been
the electric fence and the burning of charcoaled still-lifes,
villages collapsing into the tractor

and its elbows. Miami cried for one day,
then got over it. Now, Mpumalanga
and Christmas, I kick over

your niece's gift, searching for the bathroom light.
On your brother's mattress, I have trouble
with the moths. When their wings cross the curtain,
I want to wake you.

We must say: You ran
to America. You ran back. Or: Cassiopeia,
tying her intestines into an orchid,

loves the jellyfish more than her mother.
After all, your hips are incantatory, they turn us
into adults. And Mars

(I can tell, even through the ceiling),
doesn't favor this sky.

Cartulary: A Cape Town Legend

So incredibly slow. Georgia was not
on the crooked mattress at the center of the kitchen,
her grandfather stroking her toes. This,
no matter what you want
to believe.

The whispers,
and the mailwoman at the door
to the toolshed. And now, her mother in a red
miniskirt, digging into the ceiling with a soup spoon.
Georgia turns her back, her pants still
cuffed above the ankle, and coins of olive polish
go from dry to wet, ruining the fingers
of her grandfather. He remembers

his birth, biting at his cuticles, hearing
the creak of his mother's hips, the mail slot, the magazine
about sailboats, the lobster that the diver speaks of
even more than the chum, and the one
drop of blood, escaping from a fingernail or scale.
He hears water spilling from a potent aquarium

where a sperm whale is trying to hold in
her calf, proves that water can be bitten.
Thickening to ruby, the whale is a flourish of milk.

He hears the applause, slack as a *koeksister,* in Georgia's chest,
the polish loosening like oyster skin
at her feet. The crooked velocity in the spring
that solves a small white bed. The one
crashing down on his spine. Euphoria is

the obligation of nightmare.

Drisheen

Call it a sheep, call it a cow, serve it
with raisins and a little salt. Inflate

the casing with a forearm, yours or
your mother's, blend one serum

with another, commingle with
the animals. The stuff inside us

has a residue, something that sticks
to the filter-rib, the plane tickets

and palm trees, the champagne
in the bony flute.

Ask your mother who still,
one year later, is on the steroids,

still has that cough. Boil pudding.
Get angry. Slaughter collected

in an earth-bucket, a hair floating
on the top. You'll think it's horse,

but you'll be wrong. Here, we are not
permitted to ride what we eat.

Hold her hand, watch her
shiver beneath the blankets. Remember

the buttery white sauce and plenty
of pepper. This is common,

our tradition, our slow coming
to the table, hands clean, blood-

by-blood.

The Terza Rima Birth Dream
Keeps Us Awake Again

The window screen is lightning by the bedlamp
without a shade. The bulb reveals its breast, then
weeps wattage onto countless sheets of buckram.

Our eyes can't take it, want to cry for lost wrens,
their teeth, like baby teeth lost in the playgrounds.
The blood on jungle gyms cleansed

with your faintest fontanel. An elbow. *Cuckold, drowned.*
Your smallest finger: not the one most people
admire. I want to know this from the dream fold found

in eagle's nests, the copper wings that ripple
like bedroom curtains (hide our second acts). We
ungold our rings. We don't say *hieros gamos.* Feeble,

we fall through colonies (a pitchfork, queen bee,
an earth, our bed, a washboard) into something
pre-white: the doctor's mitt, the maiden love. We

are something in this damned hospital. Over something.

A Mourning

The yam on a spoon. Just a bite.
Something about the murder rate. Something
about a falling rand. Eat. Just
a bite. Just a yam on a spoon
in the dining room
of doves.

Necklace

The pig and the lamb scramble
for the highest branch. The pig, winning,

dies first. What can we do but eat it,
the fat attacking our tongues? This,
merely a meal, has very little to do

with art. With the picketing of the museums,
the removal of the busts of the Bushwomen,

their renderings in charcoal, oil paint, crooked
at their waists like apostrophes, an artist's
sly possession of their spines,

misunderstood bone, wishing itself
the mesquite pod that fed, then killed

the pig.

Jenny swaths her ribs
through the chutney and chews. Her aunt
refused to face the curator, was necklaced

with seven truck tires. *There's something in fire,*
Jenny says, and swallows, like all things wildfloral.

She knows it won't work. Still, after dinner,
she imagines the place where trees
thin to thread, the height necessary

to ignore pain and the retraction of skin,
the place where a contract of ghosts commingle.

There, a noose can be a scarf. Surely,
there were words stamped into the rubber tread,
a melting manufacturer, a color

or two, a date. She is full. She'll make it
to breakfast. Tonight, she'll feed

her silkworm pickled beets
so it will spin red, wonder how
to say *warranty* in Zulu. Before she sleeps

she tells me, *In every neck
is a buried wound.* Tomorrow,

she'll sew us our scars.

The Colubrid Exception (feeding on a butterfly)

We finish the warthog,
spit its tusks to the zinnias.
The earth a pit of allspice.

Hold hands while the *boomslang*
tries to hide its green bite
on the tree trunk. Only
our flashlight can find it, waiting
to kill anything that scares it.

Your brother promised
to let us sleep in tomorrow.
So we sit on the porch,
the ashtrays full, the night
so dark our hands leave

our bodies. The thunder
and the wet sister to thunder
breaking their scalps
open on the flagstone.

Forfeiture: Equal Parts Dirt and Air, 1994

The double-jointed soldier folds himself
into the crotch of the pear tree, forgets that today
is a holiday. Orange caterpillars collect
on the trunk, millions, he thinks, the passengers

in the jet overhead believe in Christo, pour
to the south side of the plane. *Don't follow me.*
With half a dead eagle each in our backpacks,
we can fly anywhere we want. *This was your idea.*

The porcupines, finally smoothed, commune
with the earth for a final few seconds. Beneath them,
the caterpillars become the peanuts the steward
wishes he could serve. Instead, *love me,*

poach the power of the human heart in a simple
syrup. Theirs are shaped like owls. Ours are shaped
like pears, the stems forced to bow. Out of this bowing, the sky
acknowledges its own color as the ejaculate of all birds.

Not the Whale: Folktale on the Blyde River

If there ever was a time for a laundress and a lamb, the time is right now. This minute!

A *sangoma* flutters her fan like a flying fish over orange water. Across the river, a construction worker's sons are eating clams. They wait for their sister to heal. *Three days at the most.* The youngest son, the one who is building castles just this side of the muck, swallows a shard of clamshell. His hands dig down to clay.

Their father has gone inside to run a wet rag and an ostrich feather over the girl's neck. She secretly wishes she could fly but knows prayers can't save them. Her stitches burn into his hands, the strings of his wife's mandolin. But the instrument is dead. The oldest son destroyed it with an obsidian sphere, as tight as the *sangoma's* bun.

She fans the water, rife with persimmon skins, to the choking son, clamshell tearing, blood beginning to run marine from his nose. A wave builds, then, twelve flying fish leap at the boy, cave in his chest like a mandolin—not the one the eldest destroyed, but the one the wife still plays, far from all water in West Phoenix, where her clothes are always clean, and for dinner, always lamb.

Simplicity Myrna

Ten years ago, we knew: A thunderstorm
eats through fatigues. Now, I need a yellow hem
dragging the kitchen floor
collecting orange pits and beetles.
Not a single lemonade stand.
This is the shucking of domesticity,
the small rotation of the blender's blade,
the crushing of ice into our drinks.

Myrna, you lost me when you lost
the belt to my bathrobe. How can I be
expected to serve, and why would the bosses
eat their glazed turnips from a breastplate?
I need a return to the kind of delicacy
that comes from stirring
the *beurre rouge.*

(Your physical experiment with the stockings
fell short of the proof, and the cow costume
stays in the closet). Admit it:

It's time to carry
their patio furniture into the garage, tell Leslie
to dismantle the mango stand. It's cold
and a seven-year-old with a broken arm
is such a strange thing: a toothpick
anchored into cork.

This morning, we read and watched the English station:
88 more of us dead today, and you wonder
if a single grain of sand can break.
It takes more than a blanket. . . .
Tonight, a power outage
is the salve for our dreams, and, in another country,
we would pray
for the paperboy's flat tire. So please:

Open the wine and pour. Pour like skin
and lamplight, realize: When I'm scared,
I need your cotton. When it rains,
Einstein's umbrella.

A Bad Summer for the Egoli Exhaustress

I am not drifting through the darkened house
where light larks through the tongue of aspen trees.
The light is white, but she can't move to douse
Katie in milk. Do Petrarch's dying geese
curl up beneath her lawn chair, bite her cast,
sign feathered names that we can't understand?
She's tangled with her spoon, and tastes the last
of Tuesday's maple yogurt. I should hand
her blankets. I should hand her back her knee.
Yesterday, she swore she saw it capping Petrarch's sun.
The geese extend their sleep, their filigree
of flight, and eat Katie—the largest one.
You know: It's what we have to do just to turn to steam.
My sister, it's just the cripple's favorite dream.

Nursery

Katie tugs herself from the jacaranda's cuff and her hair
      drags mud. When she
rights herself, she sees in leaf's reflection that her hair was
      always this way. Purple.
Yellow, along with the twelve buried colors, was just a
      memory.
But then, a kingfisher—the one from her mother's
      wallpaper—bores
a tiny hole in her gauze. She grows a fat bruised worm
      from between
thumb and forefinger. It's enough to feed an entire flock
of kings. It's enough to feed an entire bedroom. She
      wonders if
memory sloughs from imagination like old paint. Below
      her, far
enough that they look like rain, she hears an
      undetermined number
of schoolchildren ring the tree, singing in clumsy chorus.
      Their vocable sounds
to her like *The seemingly inanimate is animate and drives the*
      seemingly animate! La, la,
la . . . In the treetops, the moon is growing a chain saw.

The Hand Makes It Talk

The ardent lamb, pricked
by April, begins to bleed.

Douw says, last night, while he pushed
the garlic into its skin, it spoke to him,
told him, Marie Antoinette
liked onion rolls for breakfast. Last night,

he said, the animal had the fingers
of an aristocrat, until
he cut them off,

explaining the nature of heartache.
Here, we must be plants under glass, slowly
going mad with Joseph Conrad.
The boats in our blood,
let out coiling, the flamed
chakra of the oars we drop.
The ocean has taillights.

I am afraid for no reason,
looking for kisses in sleep.

What can we do but slice the lamb
into sixteenths, sacrifice its liver
to Cygnus? Here, the sky
is the nocturnal hunter of the swan,
and none of us will sleep tonight. Nieces, nephews.
Certainly not Douw with his edible
spill of beard, his bedtime verses
chiming with recipe:

1) Stork Man, beloved, let him face the thoroughness of
his scars.
2) Stop the pressure at the floating rib.

Your mother carves the cake,
buries her heart in the frost.
I love you, but I can't listen
to him anymore. I don't care if he's
your brother. We must say: with each bite
another execution,
another egg . . .

This city's dummy is waking us
to the alarm. Opening the last unfarmed door,
this after-dinner mint, this ventriloquist
with the broken arm.

Follow

They took Katie to the toolshed today,
cleaned her of her fingers. She shouldn't
have stolen the oranges. The machete

and the flint fire, hands cut and burned
closed. Orange. Purple. The sky
or us healing. Dying.

Heartbeat heartbeat heartbeat. The hay
they use to stitch up. Keep
our insides inside. She can't

play rugby today, makes a doll
from a can of condensed milk.
Gives it a voice. Something

to follow. A leopard yawning,
an impala collapsing
into calfhood. When she was smaller,

a different school, she watched
The Wizard of Oz with a rich man's daughter,
a living room that had brown carpeting

and smelled of limes.
This sort-of rain is coming, thin yarns
spooling from the sky. Katie says

she will climb one with remembered fingers
all the way to green palaces
and hearts that run on batteries.

Tonight, wet, scabbing, she says,
as if in instruction, *Click your heels
three times,* three times, they break.

Ichthyaria

Patricia, the netting of a fish here
is not as easy as you think.

We walk on a bridge of yellow leaves
when we find a bluefish that looks

like Queen Elizabeth. Surely, her lipstick
is blood, decades-old blood wiped

from the guillotine with a linen napkin,
that the gasping for air is,

like a diamond, part of the show,
the curtain falling. Her tail, you say,

is Olympic, unearths a swimming
pool from autumn, a coffee table on which

to play canasta with the fingers
of Sudanese boys. Jesus,

Patty, can't you distinguish
between hemispheres? A fillet knife

and an eyelash? It's time to close
the textbook and carve a bit of context

just below the fin. You tell me the joke
about the fishlips and the candle, but lost me

in the wax. I'm too hungry to laugh
and you are too historical. The tattoo

of Vermeer on your ass explains this, but not
the nature of paint. For that, we must

call on the lipstick, the royal blush
of monarchic lethargy, the clay

that sticks to the jacks. Ask
Vermeer. He is where he belongs.

So please, P, upend the glass eye
and the hyperventilation, slide a queen

into the krill, the white vinegar
brine. When you pray for her life,

cut the deck, and the shit. When you
pull your hands apart,

really pray.

A Diamond in the Henhouse

You say it without breakfast
and shame on you. A machine

is a machine is death. And food, maybe.
Cars that run on gunpowder. A rifle's

itching speed. We need our screens
to keep the bugs out. A boiling egg

has always made you crazy, brought you
to the brink of waterlessness.

"Without water," you say, "I am more
and more flesh."

Elegy for the Coffee Bean

From Venezuela. Or Sumatra. Something
ending in an A. Someplace that grew big-hipped
women who discuss love over lunch. Lunch would
be a river and root vegetable. No need for
windows. One day, one of the women—the one
who always tied the scarf over her
blue hair—would catch a passing dove in her right hand.

If I saw it, or you saw it, we would have thought of
baseball, of a robbed home run. But not here. Here, the
dove's mouth scatters a rain of beans. Each one black, and
divided lengthwise by a shallow split, like a loaf of bread
bursting with oven heat.

The woman rinses the dove in the river, but there is
no cooling the beans, or the broiler of its mouth.

Another woman in a similar scarf dares to pick up
a bean, roll it between her thumb and forefinger. Its
oil comes out onto her hands. In a rush, she sees the
village's last carrot, and the nature of exportation
that is a dove.

Down the river, a kilometer or so, the woman in
blue throws her head to the sky and sings one
syllable, over and over like beans in the cup
of my apology.

Casings

All the sausages pledge spice. A tongue
swollen with delight and coriander.
After pronouncing the names of farmers
and the oranges they grow (they fling
the leathery rind to the baboons—one segment
hit me in the back of the head!), everything,

believe me, everything comes together
in the hands of my father-in-law
sticky with oranges. His voice sticky
with brandy, the *wors*—ground pork
and oxtail, garlic and caul fat,

see-through organs, the spices black
under his fingernails as if he's been
digging in the mud, his schizophrenic son
dropping another ice cube into his glass,
the *braai* lit with fruitwood
and charcoal, splitting

hissed casings that your mother soaked
overnight in old spaghetti water.

But the colors of the pulverized seeds
in the Mason jars demand
a bigger mouth—the horn
of the white rhino, broken fenugreek,
the cinnamon rendered to sand. I choose

to help with the nutmeg, its round bark
hard as a bicycle helmet. Here,
even safety can be ground. What's wrong
with that? What's wrong with a metal grater
still sharp as it goes to rust? The television channel

breaking up in the kitchen
over an entire piglet (tomorrow's celebration)

shrouded pink beneath a lace veil. News
of a hailstorm in Durban, shattering windows
past midnight. Thatched roofs
blown apart. Another refugee

shot dead at the Zimbabwean border. The spice
so great, it kills the signal to the brain.

Orders, or, Militia Meeting Minutes

Run from the daisies
until the thaw
for sleep and breakfast.

The windowpane breaks
at twenty below, midday
in Tuktoyaktuk, leap year,

clear skies and all that wind.
The arrows wet their beds
dreaming of our legs

which we have always kept
below our hearts. The aural
sunglass of this stable-waking

reflects the space heater
for the livestock. I am unfriendly
to the earth and the paper towels

in my boots. At night, I take
my time—with no fish, because
of no fish—to stand still,

the first white puddle, unrhythmed,
and eight times I jump
into the heat of my hat.

She didn't recognize the choices
my fingers had to make
for one healthy spine and a dime bag of fertilizer.

I uncollared her behind the pony-house.
She bit me for that, made off
with the thumb and really

used it. All before adulthood.
All before the peace
exfiltrated the job market

and most of remedial thought.

Correspondents

1.

Tonight, everything corresponds.
The Southern Cross with rib cage.
Planet with mom. How easy it is

to love the untouchable
and obese.

2.

Tonight, only samp and sour
oranges. Pap burns on our forearms.
How can we kiss when we're hungry,

when the hives in our pants
are killing us?

3.

I am not saying that summer
is the sea glass, though I woke
in too many salts. Let's

join hands anyway, beg fat
to bless us with Jovian crisis.

4.

Last night, you say, Carolina
opened her egg and found
the fifth ocean. What a way to go!

You promise, that wasn't her
who was screaming.

5.

If we steal, take Ashley's
advice: Drink long
into morning. Hide

the mouthful
in fishbone.

6.

Tonight, we are correspondents.
Let's fall in love with the sores
in our mouths, everything red

and stellar. If we are the product
of a born-again Andromeda, we can breathe
underwater. It will come true:

Say it into my ear. Today, we eat
the elephant. Jupiter doesn't complain.

Last Letter

My daughter only wants to come home
and cook barbecue.

Pull pork. Roast spareribs.
She wants to use my mother's

recipe. The one
with the yellow mustard.

But somewhere, in a place
now known only as

overseas, she has lost her shoes.
This is very bad. What can she do

but imagine, her scream threading
the streambed like a dog

trailing its leash—not a hand anchored
to it, but a gold bust

of Shakespeare, his own tongue imagining
its place between toes?

The alluvial lottery inherent
in the arch of your foot

rests somewhere at the bottom
of an Afghan stream.

This much,
I know.

I'm sorry for the problems
with gasoline.

In anticipation of gunfire, imagination
must evolve, become musical.

You taught me this.
Of course,

this does not mean that rhyme
demeans the ankle's rake, laid

ladylike on the pinkening sand.
And, while we're at it, let's tell

all motherless soldiers to get
a motel room, the grinding

of their teeth resurrecting Rossini
and his broken rib. I want to tell her

to use it, to bow the violin, to pick
the dark meat from the carcass

with red-painted nails, slivers
of dusky punctuation smearing

the pages with periods.

I promise I will mention nothing
of the letter Z, the word

dear. I promised. But in the mornings,
I can hear her.

Not only at night anymore.
With every empty fork.

With each glass of milk.
Please, baby,

don't cry. In your strength lies
all the good music. I implore you:

Bet me that Shakespeare
didn't hide a clove of garlic

in his tights, that your father
didn't love you. Sometimes,

we all need to keep quiet
and sulfuric. I want to take you

to the place where we can pick
strawberries with our toes,

drain them of their champagne,
slip them into the mouths

of foggy husbands. But I understand:
In fighting, we erode the shrew,

we burp the things that break us.
In this, I will take all who kill you

away. We will go to Victorian waters
barefoot, and leave on stilts. Here,

the things we walk on will be perfect.

Chokecherry

Soup it
with lemon zest, cassia,

a little corn flour.

Feed it
to your daughter as punishment—

she cried today

when you brushed the knots
from her hair,

she brought home a boy

who unslung one overall
from his left shoulder

forcing his clavicle

into your living room—the one
you work the night shift for.

Allow her mouth

to know fierce
and voice that can be

ghost or television,

Grandpa or Geronimo. Both used
these fruits in pemmican,

preserved dried meat together

our ancestors and our offspring.
The mouth knows

these wooden teeth, a tongue

so furred with astringency
that the roof cleaves, the *throat*

warhorse with swallowing these red Bullies.

They say they are as wild
as *indigenous,* but we all know

what was turned into jelly—

the love formula of doctors who deliver
and nurses who clean us up.

Spoon it
over your weak liver

and celebrate

its shrinking, this cherry heart
made of smoke

keeps us alive by burning.

Ceremony

Even the glass of water on your nightstand
                              is worried about tomorrow.
A medicinal session. A needle and thread.

Some things get better

some things get worse. Orloff says,
to kill the kingfisher, you must prepare
                              to kill the king.

Prepare: like a meal, a frybread,
a ceremony for a baby at the bottom
                              of a canyon, the Havasupai

welcoming because
                    you went to school
with their medicine man.
Maybe we should have tried this
                              first. Where the heat

is carefully handled. Before the alarm clock
sixes paint your water

red, ignite
an air conditioner. An important
                              sleep. Try: the nightstand

submerged in a lake, goldfish
swimming from the drawers.

                         And: This lake
is wetter than others. Or: Your nightstand
is a cardboard box.

Rumi's Femur Found in Kruger National Park!

Rumi took off his bathrobe
And heard his hair, his arms growing.
And if to detail is to allow a mermaid legs,
We must press our faces to the water and cry into it.

Brownband cockroach—wings were fins were dream—
Noses his kitchen floor, Afghani apartment
With a spiral staircase. He forgot, like the rest
Of us, about Persia and sap, pooling its chastity, its lock.

Your father, I certainly know, was never
One to swim. He lost his keys in the shallows
To drive and open and leave
Apprentice to the chlorinated singers.

As they say in Morocco, he forgot the spin
Of the Sufi, the yellow infestation of dust to fingertip.
Love, the impossible feather and note
Cramped in the temperature of Paradise.

Kira says, "He made a mess of the house,"
Her elbows cross-tied for travel.
Wrapped in paper, her cholera
Does her writing for her.

The immediate Malatian giraffe
Paints couplets along its neck, can't reach
To tattoo its ankle with the adder.
Kira uses her nail polish and a mizzenmast . . .

The allergic Malatian giraffe
Sneezes in seaworthy fever.
Resins of formaldehyde formalize
The heart. Kira tells her husband to get dressed.

The desperate Malatian giraffe
Shoots the elephant for its tusks.
Underneath this desert,
Its brine pirates us like a maypole,

But our fish leave for the biology of winter,
Give to the piano our bloody hands.

Jo'burg Flytrap

You make your list for the market
in Burgersfort—coffee, bread,
lime. Anything fermentable.

Last night, you dreamed
her hands on you, cold as Pluto,
pulling you from the mattress
to the low grave beneath
the trampoline. You heard her

say again, *He's buried there*
in the shadows of perpetual
toy eclipse, a thing
that your nieces jump on,
pretending to be astronauts.

Since you never celebrated Halloween,
you can't understand the novelty
of costuming, and the unwrap-
ability of all sweet things.

How she has the burn scars again
the ones that, when awake,
you painted. The places where the rubber
has fused with skin, an eyepatch
with threads, the spider emptied
of her web. These things are outer-
space, gravity-defying things.

I tried to sleep next to you,
but your brother's mosquitoes
kept me up. And the long drive
in the morning. This shopping to do.
Where we're always recognized.

When you fold the list
into your pocket, you ask the ghost
why she is crying. Why she doesn't haunt
Plett Bay, a place of strawberry garnishes
and straws that twist.

When we start the car, the radio
tells us. There are reasons
the country is a crab.
There are reasons the crab is a hermit.

Via del Piede

To hold a pear by its stem
is to commune with the French
Revolution, and its heads. To eat
the pear from the bottom up

is to do what Rubens did
(a thick-necked man,
proving the world

wasn't top-heavy). Fruit is always easiest
when rendered in wax—
the empire, like everyone else, will
stand behind the velvet rope. Even they

can't break the glass without drawing
their blood, their knuckles
as skinny as a sandal. The peasants

called Holy Rome *The Big Marble
Foot*, painted their streets with tar
and reopened their fruit stands.
Flavio would do forty push-ups

before selling his first pear, contemplate
the border between the rind
and the meat. One continent away, pears

and prediction, skin divorcing itself
from the flesh, the pupil hiding
in a mustard seed. In Franschhoek, at *L'Ecole
Maternelle*, they read that in wartime

Aztec sacrifices were called flowers,
and those who were sacrificed

were also called flowers.

Another Cleopatra

That bowl of mangoes was taken
from your grandmother's Kurt Weill record

Life, Love and Laughter. The banana
proves the mango: an empty peel
and taped-together photos. *Sangomas*

who walk on coals always wear gloves.
The burns touch. A concrete floor

cracking with centipedes. Sometimes, a shoebox
is as much a home
as the river.

A line of glass jars, holes
punched into the gold lids

with a bottle opener. Twelve-packs
of strawberry-lime wine coolers.
If they get out, they will

make for the water bowl, the food collecting
in livery crumbs at the bottom.

And what if

your niece killed nothing?
Her head full of primary barrettes

and orange sun! A dropped chocolate
melting in the grass. Biologically,
any shark beached in Cape Town

owes its fin to Nandi's Cafe.
I know a domestic named Trinity Pitsou

who pissed on cursed grass
to neutralize it, her *sangoma*
who shaves her armpits

with a cobra tooth. Love how she marries
sweat and venom. Curse

and the earth. Surely, all of us
would have poisoned tongues
from using them to laugh,

bouncing the muscle in our mouths
while older worlds stay quiet.

The Parrot is Long-Grain Rice

1.

The African Gray
who talks back.

I feed him a mouthful of dish detergent
just to get my facts straight.
He vomits quarters so I can go
to the laundromat. We've always had
this understanding. For more than seventy years.

2.

Our son's dead now, but that's not
our fault. Maybe, all the time,
he was the parrot in his green
jacket, wings like his windbreaker
at the bus stop.

3.

In the middle
of the night, my wife wakes up and says,
Dimes falling from the sky, dimes
into puddles after a storm, finally
a proper coda to the rain.

4.

Seventy years, I say.

We're old, she says, dimes
will get us nowhere.

5.

When I was young, she says, dimes
allowed me feathers, my own cage
with the door closed, and a sign that said,
Knock first.

Yes, I say,
the flight story

Obsidian Death Mirror (Wakes up on a mountain of leaves and realizes the world is beautiful)

Even the asphodel
is edible. To where could they go

but the rope? (Carved verses on the back
presented to the body.)

Even today,
they will tell you: After the merchants

were pressed for their juice, dessert
was never the same.

Canaries

A lens of whale oil supports the soil. You say,
It's been this way for centuries.
I say, Yesterday, on Channel One, they lowered

a humpback into a coal mine to determine
the quality of its air. You say, The human lung
can hold only six liters of breath, which is nothing

compared to the Indian Ocean. At night here,
the water howls like a shot blesbok, one thousand
sled bottoms scraping ice in a town that's never

seen snow. You pilot me to the super-single
mattress and, of course, I can't breathe too well.
You say, Intone your tongue into a square knot,

without stain or blemish. You only talk this way
when wearing an unbuttoned blouse, devil's claw
in your hair and a cup of buchu juice on the nightstand.

We unhinge ourselves from Durban, we are silent
streets given over to mud. Where
are the headlamps when you need them? Your brother

took them into the mine. You say, Whales
are the canaries of the ocean. This sounds strange
with your tongue in my ear. Like a doorbell.

Like a hair-dryer socket. Like the kiss
in the mineshaft. We hold bellies and wish
the world to eat whale. We open bellies

and roll the canary's egg over the TV pillow's
corduroy. When we hatch, you say, our mouths
are filled not with teeth, but toothpicks. *This*

is a world without hors d'oeuvres. Have we hatched—
pigs from pig egg, lungs pinked to munificence?
When we're hungry, we breathe, night-plate dark

as a leaf. Tonight, we're having nature for dinner.
Tomorrow, we'll question our hearts, follow
the beat, like an elevator, down to the wild

swimming things who act as sentinels
for this love.

Santa Marta Fifty Miles South

Washing buckets and bales of hay, the children
mash bananas into their milk, mothers crying
for more. Never fish at the market. Crack the sun
like an egg. This morning, its shell is our city. Peel
Knysna like an orange. Save the rind for the dog.

Katie drinks the coconut, then frames herself,
hangs herself above the minister. Once
every fifty years, she will cry blood and the children
will collect it in the buckets. She wears her gold
like an angel. Tomorrow, God, they say. Today,
the horses. Behind the church, Rethabile reads
a book on whales.

A Blip in Nature

Soap collects like sand at the Kalahari's tile.
The baobab marks the drain.

Three-hundred-fifty-some kudu-prints
jump from the sand as surfacing air, taking
blister form and popping in a mock
of oxygen and landscape. Their bite-marks

spackle the agave, ribbed like a cob pulled
of its corn. These kudu—possibly Paleozoic, possibly
postmodern—drank here once, their winter
branch antlers warding off the scorpions. Their eyes,

brown as marble, wet as soap, would have looked
to the sky's receding hairline, peeling back
in orange forehead rolls, for answers: Why are we
here? And, more important, What can we eat?

Surely, there's water to be found. Surely,
there is a purpose to this calm mess of red
sand, forever swirling as water, counter-
clockwise, down the throat-pipes of a higher

but inexplicable order.

Drum Water

Like milk. Like detriment. We wake surrounded
by cones. Our eyes like goatskin
stretching over eucalyptus. Flip them over. Read
our labels. *Made in Guinea.* No name, but allow
the smell to clear the throat. Like streets,
the milk.

You ask the foreman to push dynamite
into your nightgown. He fades into his headlamp.
A red bra doesn't guarantee anything here.

Like the sink that lends us our treble. The shower
that opens our snares. You ask me

about the orange lights, why they never decided
to be suns. At a certain point, I say, it's a matter
of degrees. You assure me you're not
speaking about paper. I assure you, I speak only
of ink. And suns.

I can barely remember yesterday, when our hips
came together in calligraphy. If a letter, Z (Go back
to sleep). If a tool, a handsaw (Baby . . .). If a sound,
the tomato falling into the knife.

Camera

This morning, on my way to the bathroom, I found
the mopani worm your niece stepped on,

its opened-up belly spilling ticks. I can only imagine
the streak it left on the sole of her foot,

a swipe of black silk like corn smut. Greasy.
If I close my eyes, the coconut palms could be

an interstate, strung on the bright air
of engineering. Outside the window

over the toilet roll, Douw beats the dog
with a frond. If we track the trails of snakes,

what would we find? A vulture wearing
the head-skin of a buffalo, the only crepe stand

in town that serves blueberries. Not a single
newspaper in sight, the news a drying patch

of blood in the flattened tallgrass. Something heavy
lay here once. A long knife for splitting

coconuts, its milk purchased with a clammy coin.
Still the profile of the queen. Can you feel

the strength of her teeth, and the smoke that comes
from between them? I touch the dresses

hanging on the line, the metal springs of the clothespins
warming in the sun. In my wallet, the picture of us

in the airplane you dreamed was going to crash.
The layover in Madrid, the terminal pigeons

shitting in our hair as we slept on the bolted-
together chairs. Beyond the property line, the veldt

dips and I have to tighten my shoes. For years
we traded these photographs, bought expensive stamps

and wet their backs. This is our last
communal camera. Our spit, like the handles of the hammers

in the shed where Trinity sleeps, luminesces.
Silkworms huddle near the box fan that keeps

you sleeping, but there are insects to keep me awake.
I know they won't land on our skin—

all that spray—but the way they lotion the window screen,
exploring each way out, itches. My chest

is dripping. A mosquito makes sure of it.

Bernice's Bad Habits

You hide your tastes in other tastes. Apple
in chicory, corn in spearmint. You can't

go through life like this. Your house
is an outlet. Once, I electrocuted myself

on a bedframe, couldn't let go of the doorknob.
The nun was going to get in trouble

for moonlighting with the shofar. She said:
Tonight, electrocution is sin.

I swore
my teeth would ignite, turn to chalk,

bury themselves into an ash leaf. B,
remember this, and get it right next time:

chicory with corn—the unattainable
in the palpable.

For Omelas, My Lovebird

Pixie dust is the product of dusty pixies, shut up
in medicine cabinets with only their love

to drink. This is what we have to do in the Western
World. Ask Ursula K. Le Guin. She knows.

How aspirin goes dry in the mouth, a communion
wafer and, if you let a pixie out,

it will surely eat through your stomach
to the peephole. Allow your liver to spy

on your aunt, undressing in the guest room.
Wouldn't you? You've never lived in a coffee can,

have you? I can tell by the melon in your hair.
In Soweto, mud is the treasured shampoo, and eight-

year-olds break each other with lamp bases
over the richest handfuls. They have ivory

on the brain. Some argue that Rimbaud's sister
was the first pixie. They say she was the first

to snap clothespins onto her nipples. Some argue
that Baudelaire's lice is responsible for the dead

cornfields and for poverty. Above a certain latitude,
the clothespin kills the lice: This is lavender's

catalyst. Below this latitude, the lice keep
their cool, eat into the clothespin, and spit

its splinters into the mud. These are the richest
handfuls. Here, to exfoliate is to change your color.

In one sense, you float like a pixie from the clothesline
with sore wings. In another, you hang like a shroud.

Someone dead will have to wear you,
while in Turin, the blind scientist

tries to enter the closed museum.

Hunger

Gertie is dead. The pig, hide like a suit
of pennies, is dead.

Fuck you. You will never
bury that pig.

You cry beautifully,
knees skinned like a bell pepper.

It is the pain
with the most beautiful voice
that is the cruelest.

Mazisi's Widow

He was a big man
with a lot of feelings, but I saw him
break.

A Styrofoam cup, filled
halfway with milk, wants only to be
barley. Planted, sewn.

His wife's
lace hem collects garlic skins,
breadcrumbs from the kitchen floor.
She prepares me her peri-peri
chicken livers, says, *We had*

the courage to lead our lives well,
openly, and like pigs. She must
be referring to munificence
and roses. Now she lives
in the toolshed, paints the picture
she couldn't paint before: a horse
with the breasts of a woman, Janus-
faced and birthing.

It's been fourteen months since Mazisi died.
They buried him with a black mamba
and a cream tube of acrylic paint. When
the venom becomes too much,
she opens the window,
then opens the window
a little wider.

Two Weddings

I love you and, if somewhere else, you'd wring
the rooster, toss its comb to your pile
of cousins (the origin of the rubber band).

They would exchange their clothes
for potatoes. Aunt Becky screams, "Awake!
Awake!" from the deep end of her wheelchair,

and your mother thumbs her bookmark (H. D.
says, *your Holy Ghost was an apple-tree*).
I'm trying to concentrate, Honey, to become

one of the essential population (the horror
of the grin, six rows of teeth), but your side
of the family coughs like a pig, and I can see it

in the friar's eyes (his rendezvous with the toad).
They're planting us like walnuts (cherry,
olive), saving our milk for the sick. We have

to eat our bread in front of someone religious, otherwise
your father will steal it (six years ago, an adder
ate his earlobe). This all and this altar

bear the stink of unripe cherry (wild strawberries
produce a low fertilizer). The wind kicks
like a mule kicking an oil drum (eaten by bees

to feed the wolf), and dysentery crosses
an ocean. Your cousin—the one with the sore
throat—shouts about the diamond (an infant

cast in silver), and even the friar laughs (money
is smoke through the stones), jokes about hearts
and barometers (no window, no chimney).

The mosquitoes watch, parallel to the pond,
holding their danger for the declaration (a chemical
improbability). Malarial, your parents clap and cry, mine

cover our feet like leaves (soft, cool, a stick
in the guise of a tombstone). When they rot,
they are (finally) wild. Let's vow to make children,

to eat, sleep, and die in the same
room. I ring your finger (winnow). In Mpumalanga, a goat
falls from its mountain.

Not Mary

Fifty times I call you back
from the lion, and fifty times
you recite *baobab, baobab* . . .

Again you assure me, in death
is this medicine, a dusty head of hair
stringing mazes of prey over dustier
shoulders.

When you break, your nose
bleeds aloe. When you convulse,
I soften my hands. It is so difficult
to imagine snow when the bush
is an eyebrow and smoke.
It is so difficult to finish imagining.

When the succulents petrify,
finish your meal. When you empty, want.
I want you to fall to your knees,
clasp your hands like a fish kiss.
Here there are no fish, only a girl
falling to her knees, clasping her hands
like dead bells.

Elegy for Simon at the Cape of Good Hope

I hope that, for the rest of your days,
you don't have to worry about wolves—
one is for the gray, two for the red, and so on
and so on, until we arrive at the packed
heart, the beat lost in the whistle.

You never saw Africa. Your one continent
undone like a shoelace. Even a thread
has two sides, and its bow avoided us both.

But you know what port wine tastes like
in Newark, the scattered bartender from
a four-syllable town outside Lisbon, wiping
his moustache like a paradise flycatcher,
drying his wings and buying us a round.

He played your music. That song about Carlos
and his scar, the eel swimming like Caesar
over his belly.

Tonight, the knife fights of the world
stop short of the stabbing.

No one wants blood, except your fingers,
your eight-hundred-dollar guitar,
the fish we taste like leopards, like all things
sustainable by gold. We live
under their tongues—

in Cape Town, Table Mountain loses
its fourth leg, and spills forty stones.
You would have called the thirty-ninth
manganite, and would have been wrong.

But the way you would have strummed it,
fingernails way too long, magnetic,

the waves—white, then blue-white—
howling in defiance

tonight, against latitude.
Like each animal,
thick as a ribbon, some planet, we hunt, you die,
unspool your rock like cantata.

If music is the crooked announcement
of our continental scars, no one will listen. You know:

No one
ever listens.

Notes

Warranty in Zulu began as a project to explore the ways in which the exhibits of South African museums and galleries have changed since the fall of apartheid in 1994, documenting how the "landscape" of the South African art scene has changed in style, substance, and accessibility with the sociopolitical landscape, with the aim of uncovering a larger statement about the interaction between politics and aesthetics. After numerous trips to South Africa, my wife's homeland and her family's country of residence, the project became laced with the personal, the various narrators herein (many inspired by unofficial interviews, casual conversations, and folklore) engaging issues of history, identity, confused observation, the nature of healing, irrational fear, irrational love, and the collision between insider and outsider voices. While not every poem in the book is set specifically within South Africa (most are), each struggles with similar thematic strains.

"Four Hours to Mpumalanga":
- Mauritz Naude, manager of the National Cultural History Museum in Pretoria, South Africa, recently declared that a number of museums are still busy rewriting their exhibits. The Sasol Art Museum at the University of Stellenbosch challenged previous conventions with their exhibit entitled *After Apartheid: Nine South African Documentary Photographers*. These photographs by such artists as Zwelethu Mthethwa and Jenny Gordon, embody a militancy and sense of native triumph unavailable in South African museums prior to 1994.
- Bulawayo is the second largest city in Zimbabwe.
- Burgersfort is a large town in the Mpumalanga Province of South Africa.

"Father-in-Law Agitprop" and "Nursery":
The kingfisher:
- Symbol of peace and abundance.

- If killed, and its body sundried, it is believed to be a talisman to repel thunderstorms and lightning.
- In the world of bird expression and song linguistics, it is known for concision and clarity.
- It is contemplative and needs its space.
- Some believe its large head indicates an abuse of ego. This is a teaching tool.

"Favor":
- Cassiopeia is meant to evoke the constellation and the vanity of the mythical queen, which angered the sea god Poseidon, and resulted in her downfall, as well as the Cassiopeia jellyfish, whose flower-shaped organs are visible through its body. *Of what is a hemisphere made?* The arrogance of the questioning may result in the downfall of the poem's speaker. Possible, and futile guesses: The sky? The ocean?

"The Terza Rima Birth Dream Keeps Us Awake Again":
- *Heiros gamos* is Greek for "holy marriage," often referencing the union of god and goddess.

"Necklace":
- The South Africa Museum in Cape Town recently removed their Bushmen exhibit. According to Naude, the exhibit apparently upheld the previously tolerated notion that black South Africans were a "strain of subhuman."
- Necklacing is a form of capital punishment that has been exacted for various reasons—theft, crossing a picket line, not supporting a particular cause, etc.—in which the victim's hands are bound and a car or truck tire filled with gasoline is wedged over his or her head and set ablaze.

"Not the Whale: Folktale on the Blyde River":
- In 1864, the Swazi fought the Mapulana along the Blyde River Canyon. Bone fragments of those killed are still wedged into the rock crevices there.

- A *sangoma* is a Zulu (or Ndebele, Swazi, or Xhosa) medicine woman, healer, spiritual guide (See also: "Another Cleopatra").

"A Bad Summer for the Egoli Exhaustress":
- *Egoli*, which means, "City of Gold" in the Zulu language, refers to Johannesburg.

"Casings":
- The collapse of the economy, food supply, and health system, along with politically motivated violence, has forced many Zimbabweans to seek refuge in South Africa over the last ten years. Zimbabweans who flee across the border into South Africa risk rape, robbery, and brutal beatings by outlaws known as the "guma-guma." They also run the risk of being eaten by crocodiles while swimming across the Limpopo River.

"Correspondents":
- According to Zulu legend, the elephant came upon a woman carrying an ax and a cluster of sticks, and her child. Noticing the elephant, she deduced his intention and begged, "Spare my child, O Elephant!" The elephant refused. "Then," said the mother, "if this evil must occur, swallow me too, O Elephant!" So the elephant swallowed mother and child, and they found the company of all the other children whom the elephant heretofore ate. Eventually, the child became hungry, and the mother built a fire with her sticks. With her ax, she shaved away the elephant's inner flesh, cooked it, and everyone ate. The fire's burning heat filled the elephant with great pain, and he began running, the thunder of his hoofs rattling them inside as he raced over mountain and valley. Finally exhausted, he fell down dead. With her ax, the mother chopped and chopped until she opened up the elephant's side. Squeezing through his rib cage and skin, they crept out into the air and became a new nation in a new country.

"Last Letter":
- Composed in a mother's head for her daughter, fighting in a distant war. They used to bond over Shakespeare, classical music, food . . .

"Rumi's Femur Found in Kruger National Park!":
- Number Four on my list of fantasy tabloid headlines.
- The Cast: *Rumi* (Rumi); *Kira* (Rumi's second wife); *the Malatian Giraffe* (an image fusing Malatya (where Rumi's family settled when he was eight years old) and South Africa; a vision of Rumi's; a meditational tool or spirit animal to ease him out of his fish-out-of-wateriness along the South Africa - Mozambique border); *the Mizzenmast* (the seafaring tool, and perhaps the crude flotation device the couple used to arrive here, that Kira uses to alter the Giraffe's appearance after an argument with her husband).

"Another Cleopatra":
- Another strange, compelling, and artistically racist link between American history and contemporary South Africa, from the New Year's Eve Cape Town Minstrel Carnival's press release: *"Every New Year, thousands of minstrels take to the streets in a dazzling display of colourful satin uniforms, shiny parasols, painted faces and foot tapping banjo tunes that accompany the traditional folk songs, many of Cape Malay origin. The parade is known colloquially as the 'Coon Carnival' ('coon' referring to a member of a minstrel troupe). . . . The traditional event has its origins in the 19th century when minstrel entertainers on American cruise ships stopped off in Cape Town; their sounds and styles were incorporated into the New Year festivals of the newly freed Malay slaves."*

"Obsidian Death Mirror (Wakes up on a mountain of leaves and realizes the world is beautiful)":
- Found in a museum with no name.
- The asphodel, as popularized by William Carlos Williams, is the death flower.

"Hunger":

- The owners of an orange farm had a pet pig who died due to a bite from the venomous black mamba. They wanted to hold an official funeral for the fallen beast, as it was a beloved family companion. Some of the farm workers, many of whom had been subsisting solely on a mixture of cornmeal and water for months on end, protested the burial of the pig and, in spite of the poison coursing through its corpse, ate it. Not a single diner got sick.

Acknowledgments

Poems in this work have originally appeared in the
following publications, to whose editors grateful
acknowledgment is made:

Burnside Review: "In Burying the Avocet"

Cimarron Review: "Santa Marta Fifty Miles South"

FIELD: "Father-in-Law Agitprop," "Mazisi's Widow"

The Florida Review: "Two Weddings"

Fourth River: "Jo'burg Flytrap," "Another Cleopatra"

Memorious: "Not the Whale: Folktale on the Blyde River"

New Hampshire Review: "For Omelas, My Lovebird"

The New Republic: "Follow"

Prairie Schooner: "Drisheen," "Chokecherry"

Some poems originally appeared
in the chapbook *Four Hours to Mpumalanga,*
published by Pudding House Publications, 2008.

Barrow Street Poetry

Warranty in Zulu
Matthew Gavin Frank (2010)

Heterotopia
Lesley Wheeler (2010)

This Noisy Egg
Nicole Walker (2010)

Black Leapt In
Chris Forhan (2009)

Boy with Flowers
Ely Shipley (2008)

Gold Star Road
Richard Hoffman (2007)

Hidden Sequel
Stan Sanvel Rubin (2006)

Annus Mirabilis
Sally Ball (2005)

A Hat on the Bed
Christine Scanlon (2004)

Hiatus
Evelyn Reilly (2004)

3.14159+
Lois Hirshkowitz (2004)

Selah
Joshua Corey (2003)